A BASIC BOOK OF
LOVEBIRDS
LOOK-AND-LEARN

by
TAMMY HALABURDA

Photographs and Illustrations: Dr. Herbert R. Axelrod, Horst Bielfeld, Pam Biggs, S. Bischoff, M. DeFreitas, Isabelle Francais, Michael Gilroy, Fred Harris, M. Heidenreich, Horst Mayer, R. & V. Moat, Eric Peake, Robert Pearcy, John R. Quinn, H. Reinhard, San Diego Zoo, Vince Serbin, T. Tilford, Louise Van der Meid, Vogelpark Walsrode.

Cover photo of Peach-faced Lovebirds by Michael Gilroy.

Distributed in the UNITED STATES to the Pet Trade by T.F.H. Publications, Inc., One T.F.H. Plaza, Neptune City, NJ 07753; distributed in the UNITED STATES to the Bookstore and Library Trade by National Book Network, Inc. 4720 Boston Way, Lanham MD 20706; in CANADA to the Pet Trade by H & L Pet Supplies Inc., 27 Kingston Crescent, Kitchener, Ontario N2B 2T6; Rolf C. Hagen Ltd., 3225 Sartelon Street, Montreal 382 Quebec; in CANADA to the Book Trade by Macmillan of Canada (A Division of Canada Publishing Corporation), 164 Commander Boulevard, Agincourt, Ontario M1S 3C7; in the United Kingdom by T.F.H. Publications, PO Box 15, Waterlooville PO7 6BQ; in AUSTRALIA AND THE SOUTH PACIFIC by T.F.H. (Australia), Pty. Ltd., Box 149, Brookvale 2100 N.S.W., Australia; in NEW ZEALAND by Brooklands Aquarium Ltd. 5 McGiven Drive, New Plymouth, RD1 New Zealand; in Japan by T.F.H. Publications, Japan—Jiro Tsuda, 10-12-3 Ohjidai, Sakura, Chiba 285, Japan; in SOUTH AFRICA by Multipet Pty. Ltd., P.O. Box 35347, Northway, 4065, South Africa. Published by T.F.H. Publications, Inc. Manufactured in the United States of America by T.F.H. Publications, Inc.

SUGGESTED READING

T.F.H. offers the most comprehensive selections of books dealing with pet birds. A selection of significant titles is presented here; they and the thousands of other animal books published by T.F.H. are available at the same place you bought this one, or write to us for a free catalog.

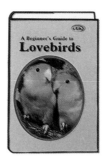

T.F.H. Publications
One T.F.H. Plaza
Third & Union Avenues
Neptune, NJ 07753

2

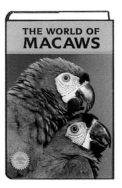

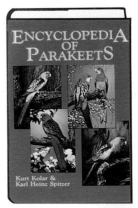

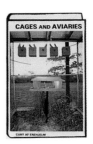

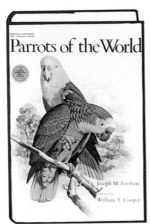

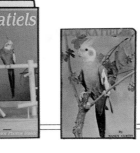

3

INTRODUCTION

The name 'lovebird' was given to these little parrots because of the affection shown between paired birds. Sometimes this bonding lasts until the death of one of the birds. This affection is not usually shown towards others but instead severe fighting occurs. ▶

This Pied Blue specimen is just one of the many beautiful color mutations of *A. roseicollis.* ▶

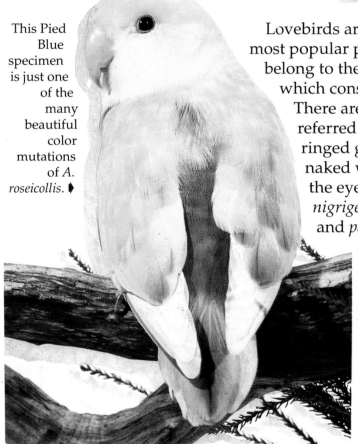

Lovebirds are one of the most popular pet birds today. They belong to the genus *Agapornis*, which consists of nine species. There are four species that are referred to as the 'white eye-ringed group' because of the naked white patches about the eyes. Some consider *nigrigenis, lilianae, fischeri,* and *personata* to be one species consisting of four subspecies. Similarities among this group are those of behavior, nesting habits, and the act of voluntary mixed matings, creating hybrids.

Lovebirds are among the smallest birds of the parrot family and their area of distribution is Africa and Madagascar. For the most part, they are hardy birds with a stocky build and a short tail. Body length is usually five to six inches and they live for over ten years.

▶ If purchasing two lovebirds, it is a good idea for both to be of the same species. A larger or more aggressive bird may bully the other.

INTRODUCTION

The basic plumage color of Lovebirds is green, but there are many mutations that occur in captive breeding programs making them available in an array of colors. Three of the nine species show sexual dimorphism.

Peach-faced Lovebirds are probably the most aggressive, but are also the most popular and widely available.

← This Masked Lovebird, *Agapornis personata*, is one of four lovebird species belonging to the 'white eye-ringed group'.

There are many reasons for the popularity of this little bird. One reason is its small size, thus requiring less space than a larger parrot. Another reason is affordability. Some variables affect the cost of the bird, such as color and whether or not the bird is hand-raised. If you wish to have a tame companion, a hand-raised bird is recommended. Lovebirds have no exceptional dietary or care needs as compared with other birds and are extremely attractive. They are also active breeders and make great aviary birds. A few of the species are very sociable and will breed contentedly among colony conditions. Their expressive and curious personalities are sure to charm anyone.

Lovebirds are very active and their comical behavior is sure to provide great pleasure. ▶

SELECTION

Prior to the purchase, the first thing you may want to determine is the type of lovebird you want. This is important for breeding purposes, but may be less important when purchasing a pet. There are three species which are commonly available, the Peach-faced Lovebird, the Masked Lovebird and the Fischer's Lovebird. A reason for their increased availability is that they are easy to breed. These would be the choice for one looking to breed lovebirds for the first time.

← Since both sexes of the Peach-faced Lovebird are alike, you cannot tell male and female birds apart at a glance.

← When selecting a lovebird, either for a companion or for breeding stock, a bit of research is a must. This will help assure that you are getting a quality bird best suited for your wants and needs.

If purchasing a bird that is not hand tame, be prepared to spend a lot of time in the process. ►

If the cages and surroundings are dirty and unkempt, there is a good chance you will want to find another place to purchase your bird. These birds are clean and seem to be in good health.

Cost may also be a factor in your selection process. Certain color-bred mutations will cost more. If you want a tame pet, it is best to purchase a hand-raised chick that is already used to human touch and companionship. These birds will be more expensive but will be worth the cost. Parent reared or older birds will be difficult to tame. Selecting a bird of about eight weeks is best. A young bird will have black on its beak which will disappear as it gets older.

◀ The Red-faced Lovebird is rather rare, harder to find, and more expensive.

When making a selection you will want to choose a healthy subject, therefore check signs for any possible sickness. It is not only important to check the bird, but also the place in which you will be purchasing that bird. Is it clean and well kept? Is the seller knowledgeable about the stock and their care?

▶ Before making any purchases, make sure you are able to care for your bird or birds properly. Be aware of the responsibilities and time involved in keeping them healthy and happy.

SELECTION

The same holds true when looking for breeding stock. Find out if there are any breeders in your area, visit with them and check out their establishment. If possible, try to purchase proven pairs, birds with a history of successful matings and offspring development. If this is not available to you, a good second choice would be to purchase pairs in which at least one bird is been proven.

If purchasing pairs for breeding, ask the seller about its breeding records. Has the hen raised chicks successfully with little or no complications?

When selecting a bird, the chest area should be full, showing no protrusion of the breast bone. This would indicate extreme weight loss.

The breeder should be able to tell you the genotype (genetic make-up) of the birds, making the outcomes of your breeding more controlled.

When making your selection, observe all birds first from a distance. This way you may be able to notice if any birds look sick. If a bird is sitting with feathers all fluffed and head down with both feet on the perch, it may be sick. A healthy bird will sleep with one foot held up.

This is a fine example of a healthy bird. It is best to avoid choosing those that have any cuts or wounds. ➤

◀ Hand-raised babies will be more costly, but are well worth it.

Obtaining true pairs may be a problem because five of the species show no sexual dimorphism. ➤

Get closer to observe the birds further. Choose one where the eyes are clear and not runny. No discharge should be coming from the nostrils and its breathing should not be labored or wheezy. Also make sure the vent area is clean. The feathers should be clean and smooth, not broken and dull and should not have any bald patches as this could indicate a more serious problem. Watch the bird to make sure it is alert and active. After all your research is done, and before you make the purchase of your new bird, it is best to have its cage already home and set up.

Don't forget to check the beak and claws to make sure they are not overgrown.

MADAGASCAR LOVEBIRD

◀ In the wild, these birds spend much time in groups, usually on the ground feeding on grass seed which seems to be their main diet.

The Madagascar Lovebird, *Agapornis cana*, also known as the Grey-headed Lovebird, is the only species that appears in Madagascar where they inhabit the brush of the open forest. It is one of the smaller species measuring 5 inches. This is one of three species that show sexual dimorphism, meaning that the male and female show phenotypic differences. The primary color is green. In the male, the head, neck, and upper breast area is a light gray and on the female, these areas are a lighter yellow-green.

After the chicks leave the nest, the male will take over the responsibility of feeding his young until weaned.
▸

It will take an experienced bird breeder to show successful results in breeding the Madagascar Lovebird. ▸

These birds are very shy and nervous. They become spooked easily and will quickly retreat to a corner or nest box. Because they are so timid they are not easy birds to breed and should be left to those with experience. If these birds are to be kept in aviaries, they should be given more privacy by surrounding it with shrubs or other plants to keep disturbances to a minimum.

Even though these birds are known to be shy, hand-raised chicks can become trustful companions. ◀

MADAGASCAR LOVEBIRD

The primary color of the Madagascar Lovebird is green, but in the male, the head, neck, and upper breast area is a light gray and on the female these areas are a lighter yellow-green. ▶

Madagascar Lovebirds are not colony nesters in the wild, so it is best to house pairs separately. If kept outside they need to have a heated area. When nesting they can use a nest box as small as one offered to budgerigars or something larger may also be used. Their nests are not that complex, they bring material to the nest tucked under their feathers to line the bottom only. Moss or a layer of rotting wood should be placed on the bottom of the nest box. It is best to leave these birds alone as much as possible during breeding so as not to frighten the hen. Madagascar Lovebirds are not readily available and probably only a few breeders have well established stock.

◄ These lovebirds will eat berries as well as seed and grains in the wild.

Notice the small gray beak; these birds have the smallest beaks of all the lovebirds. ◄

THE RED-FACED LOVEBIRD

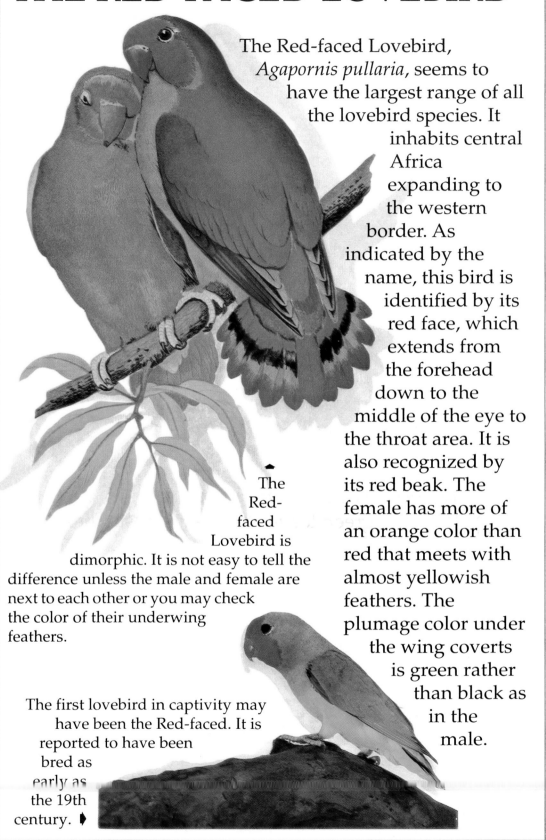

The Red-faced Lovebird, *Agapornis pullaria*, seems to have the largest range of all the lovebird species. It inhabits central Africa expanding to the western border. As indicated by the name, this bird is identified by its red face, which extends from the forehead down to the middle of the eye to the throat area. It is also recognized by its red beak. The female has more of an orange color than red that meets with almost yellowish feathers. The plumage color under the wing coverts is green rather than black as in the male.

The Red-faced Lovebird is dimorphic. It is not easy to tell the difference unless the male and female are next to each other or you may check the color of their underwing feathers.

The first lovebird in captivity may have been the Red-faced. It is reported to have been bred as early as the 19th century. ◗

THE RED-FACED LOVEBIRD

They are a timid bird that can be extremely nervous. They are definitely not a bird for the beginner. It is one of the hardest birds to breed in captivity due to its unique nesting habits. In the wild their nests are built in arboreal termite mounds. They occasionally occupy terrestrial mounds where they hollow out a burrow in which to lay their eggs.

The area these birds inhabit in their homeland are of woodland savannas and secondary forests.

These birds have very kind natures and are not argumentative.

Some breeders use bales of peat or cork to simulate a suitable area. The hens will use grass, bark, and green leaves to line the nest. These materials will be tucked into their feathers and carried back to the nest. Because they are so difficult to breed, they are quite rare. A unique feature is that it sleeps hanging upside down from its perch as the hanging parrots and parakeets.

These birds can be quite nervous. Extreme caution should be taken when bringing them into a new environment.

BLACK-WINGED LOVEBIRD

◀ In the wild, these birds are found mostly on the high plateau in habitats of open forest, preferably among juniper stands.

The Black-winged Lovebird, *Agapornis taranta*, is also called the Abyssinian Lovebird. It is found in the area of Africa known as Ethiopia.

These are the largest of the species and are generally green with the male having a red band on its forehead extending to a red ring around the eye. They have black flight feathers, brownish-black on the female, and their beak is red.

◀ ➤ Squabbles occur often between the same sex. The female (left) of this species is larger and stronger than the male (below). The male will usually seek out its mate for protection should the need arise.

◀ If these birds are provided a snug nest box, they can be wintered outdoors In their homeland the evening temperature can drop below zero.

BLACK-WINGED LOVEBIRD

Flocks may congregate to feed together on one of their favorite native foods- the fig.

They are not that common and have not really become well established among lovebird breeders. They are a fairly hardy bird that will do well in an aviary year round. Their nests are usually quite small with just a bit of material to cover the bottom.

A unique feature of this bird is that it uses its own feathers as part of the nest lining. If hand raising a young bird, it can make quite a tame and affectionate pet. They can be argumentative amongst themselves because they are very territorial. Serious fights are not common if housed in a roomy aviary.

It is easy to recognize the difference between the sexes in this species. The female lacks the red on the forehead and around the eye.

PEACH-FACED LOVEBIRD

Peach-faced Lovebirds, *Agapornis roseicollis*, inhabit a range in south-west Africa in arid, open country at elevations of about 5,000 feet. They are never far from water and are found in small flocks that feed mostly on berries and seeds. In their homeland they are often considered pests for they flock together in hundreds in some areas raiding ripening maize crops. Taking advantage of maturing crops is also true of other *Agapornis* species.

Peach-faced

One reason for the popularity of these birds are the color mutations that occur of which this is only one example.

Lovebirds are the most popular species today. This is probably due to prolific breeding habits. They will nest continually throughout the year. It is important, if keeping these birds in an aviary, that you take the nest boxes out to give them a break. They should only be allowed to raise about three clutches per year so that they stay healthy. These birds will carry nesting material to their nest in their rump feathers where they will build a cup like structure in which to lay their eggs.

PEACH-FACED LOVEBIRD

Not only are these birds the most popular, but they are also the most aggressive. If purchasing two, it is best to do so at the same time and when they are young, for they are extremely territorial. You must closely watch your couple for any signs of aggression, if this is observed, they should be separated.

Active and playful describe the lovebird. This little fellow can easily be entertained for hours disassembling its beautiful and decorative perch.

It is not uncommon for one to seriously or fatally injure a cage mate. For this reason too, breeding pairs are best housed separately. Lovebirds will even attack birds bigger than itself. One should exercise great caution if putting them in with other bird species.

Both sexes are alike in this species, making it difficult to determine breeding pairs. ➥

➥ This Peach-faced Lovebird is of normal coloring. It is distinguished by the pinkish-red head, neck, and throat area. The rump is a beautiful bright blue and the flight feathers are black. You may notice a vague ring around the eye, but it is not as prominent as those belonging to the white eye-ringed group.

BLACK-COLLARED LOVEBIRD

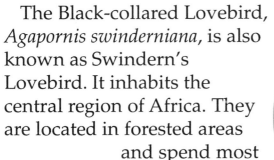

The Black-collared Lovebird, *Agapornis swinderniana*, is also known as Swindern's Lovebird. It inhabits the central region of Africa. They are located in forested areas and spend most of their time high in the treetops, where they feed mostly on figs.

◀ This is the only species that has a black beak. It also is distinguished by a black band on the back of its neck and a brownish/yellow band below that.

In specimens that have been studied, milky maize, insects, and some other grains, as well as figs, were found in their crops and stomachs. ➡

◀ There are no specimens in captivity. The reason for this is due to its specialized diet of figs. They will refuse all other foods and perish within a few days.

Since they are almost strictly arboreal, they seldom come to the ground and are not often seen.

BLACK-CHEEKED LOVEBIRD

The Black-cheeked Lovebird, *Agapornis nigrigenis*, is found in the Zambezi River valley area of south-central Africa, where it lives in lowland areas. It is said to have 'the most restricted range of the Agapornids'. Little is known of its breeding habits in the wild. These birds are available on the market and are also one of the most expensive. It seems that because they breed well in captivity they would be more available but pure birds are not common. At one time they were imported in large numbers, now they are considered endangered. Good breeding stock is hard to find and many strains have been crossed with Black Masked Lovebirds.

Black-cheeked Lovebirds are cheerful, easy going, and they get along well with others.

Male and female birds are alike in this species. The head color is brown with the cheeks and face blackish and the upper chest area an orange-red. There is no blue coloring on the rump as in other lovebird species.

This bird belongs to the 'white eye-ring' group. Notice the wide naked periophthalmic ring.

THE NYASA LOVEBIRD

The Nyasa Lovebird, *Agapornis lilianae*, is distributed in Zambia, around the Zambezi River Valley area, parts of Tanzania and Mozambique. It lives in areas of low altitude in river valleys, where large groups flock together, often spending large amounts of time on the ground by watering holes and searching for grass seeds.

The only mutation established in this species is the lutino. The head is red in color while the body is a bright yellow with white flight feathers. ▶

◀ For years this species was thought to be a variation of the Peach-faced Lovebird, which may seem strange because there are noticeable differences between the two.

The red beak makes it resemble a Fischer's Lovebird more so than a Peach-faced which has a horn colored beak. ▶

THE NYASA LOVEBIRD

Berries make up a large part of its diet but they are also found eating fruit and plant buds. Not much information is available about its breeding habits in the wild, but documentation has been made of breeding taking place in the months of January and February. The Nyasa will utilize old Weaver nests and house eaves in which to lay their eggs.

← It seems to be unknown why stock has dwindled over the years. Because of this, they are not that common and if found, are quite expensive.

Nesting material is carried in the beak rather than in the feathers as is common with most lovebird species and is usually comprised of bark and plant stalks. ▶

← Being a less aggressive group, they have been successfully bred in the colony system, but it still may be wise to separate breeding pairs.

Many times this bird is confused with the Fischer's Lovebird. The crown and forehead are an orange color fading to salmon-red around the throat and cheeks. The Fischer's has blue upper tail feathers where the Nyasa's rump is green.

FISCHER'S LOVEBIRD

This is a good lovebird species to start with because they are fairly hardy and breed well in captivity. ▶

The Fischer's Lovebird, *Agapornis fischeri*, lives to the south of Lake Victoria in the northern part of Tanzania. These birds prefer more open country such as grasslands and savannas where palm, acacia and baobab trees are present. They live in small flocks and nest in colonies in palm, baobab, and weaver nest sites.

The breeding time for these birds is during the months of May through July. Nesting material is carried in the beak and consists of flexible material such as twigs, bark, and leaves. Seeds are the main diet, especially those of acacia trees, as well as other trees and grasses.

◄ In the wild they can do great damage to crops and are sometimes poisoned or shot.

The sexes cannot be distinguished from each other by visual means. ▶

FISCHER'S LOVEBIRD

In the wild these birds will breed in colonies. ▶

◆ In captivity the Fischer's Lovebird will hybridize with others of the white eye-ringed group and also with the Peach-faced, but this does not happen in the wild.

The forehead of this bird is reddish-orange as are the cheeks and throat. The neck area turns yellow while behind the head starts the olive green coloring. The rump area is a bright blue.

◀ This is one of the three most popular species today.

MASKED LOVEBIRD

Masked Lovebirds, *Agapornis personata*, are found in the northeast section of Tanzania. Here they live in grasslands that are sparsely covered with acacia trees. Their diet and nesting habits are like that of the Fischer's, with breeding season being between the months of March and August.

◀ Species with white orbital eye rings have similar nesting habits, such as carrying nest material in the beak rather than in the feathers.

Both of the sexes are alike, having a black mask that covers the entire head region. The throat and chest area is yellow with the rest of the body being green; the rump area is blue. They are one of the most numerous species available.

◆ The periophthalmic ring group will hybridize in captivity with each other and also with *A. roseicollis*, but it has been mentioned that this latter breeding will produce sterile offspring.

In this species, the male will help the female in the nest building activities. ▶

MASKED LOVEBIRD

◀ The female of this species will only leave the nest box during incubation to eliminate waste and to feed. Many times the male will feed the hen in the nest box.

The first mutation to be established was the blue variety. Here the mask stays blackish but the yellow chest and throat area has been changed to white and the green plumage to blue. The bill has changed from red to horn colored.

Masked Lovebirds will nest in small crevices or hollows in the wild, but larger nest boxes in captivity are suggested. They build a cup-like nest, filling up almost the entire cavity with long strips of bark, and line it with softer materials such as feathers, grasses and twigs.

◀ Masked Lovebirds will breed year round, like the Peach-faced, but should only be allowed to do so from the spring till fall. Rearing only three clutches per year is advised.

◀ Not only is there a blue mutation, there are also lesser established ones such as yellows, albinos, cinnamons and pieds.

Because they can be fairly aggressive, breeding pairs should be placed in separate roomy aviaries, although some have success with breeding them in colony set-ups. ▶

MUTATIONS

The definition of a mutation is a variation or change in hereditary character. A gene is a chemical unit in a chromosome that carries a specific sequence of information, which makes up a hereditary trait.

It is not fully understood why genes mutate but this is the reason for the different colors observed. In the wild these mutations are generally lost, unless it proves advantageous to the specimen. In this case, the bird may evolve to add that character or become a separate or sub-species.

◄ The blue mutation of the Masked Lovebird was the very first mutation available. The bird on the right is a Yellow Masked.

The Fischer's Lovebird has a yellow mutation. ▶

◄ This is a Dutch Blue Peach-faced Lovebird.

◀ This color variety of the Peach-faced Lovebird is called a Silver Cherry.

◀ This beautiful bird is an American Pied Light Green, a very popular Peach-faced variety.

◀ Most color mutations occur in the Peach-faced Lovebird.

The only mutation available in the Nyasa Lovebird is the Lutino pictured on the left, the bird to the right is a normal Nyasa. ▶

◀ There is no doubt that in the future, other mutations will become available.

The Peach-faced Lovebird on the left is an orange mutation while the one on the right is normal. ▶

MUTATIONS

◀ This beautiful yellow bird is a Lutino Peach-faced.

This Cremino Peach-faced is a sex-linked color variety. ▶

◀ Notice the light beige color of the flight feathers, distinguishing this bird as a Cinnamon Peach-faced variety.

◀ The lack of color distinguishes this bird as an American White Peach-faced.

MUTATIONS

◀ Pictured here are a White and two Lutino birds of *A. roseicollis*

The breeding of a Pied Dutch Blue and a Yellow will create the American Pied White. ◀

In captive situations, through careful and knowledgeable breeding, it is possible to sustain and reproduce characteristics normally found in wild lovebirds. If interested in breeding for color mutations it is best to get a better understanding of basic genetics. This will allow you to predict certain outcomes of specific matings.

◀ This attractive blue mutation is dubbed Cobalt.

◀ Shown here are examples of the Cinnamon Slate and Cinnamon Blue strains of *A. roseicollis*.

CAGES

There are many suitable cages for lovebirds on the market today, as compared with a few years ago when most lovebirds were kept in smaller cages built for budgerigars. It is best to purchase the largest cage that you can afford because these birds are very active and need room for exercise.

When selecting a cage, be sure that it is suitable for lovebirds. If you purchase a very large cage built for a macaw, you will see that it is very spacious but the bar spacing will be too wide and your bird will be able to come and go as he pleases. Look at how the wire is situated. The bars should go horizontally, as well as vertically, to allow your bird the ability to climb up and down the sides of the cage. The best type of cage would be a simple rectangular model, allowing more length than height to provide the bird with some flight space.

▲ Some cages come with playpen tops that have perches and ladders, giving your bird an unconfined play and exercise area.

You will need at least one water dish and one food dish, but it is best to have three or four different dishes—one dish for fresh foods and treats, so as not to soil the seed mixture, and one for gravel or grit. Last but not least, don't forget to include a ladder, swing and a few toys for these playful creatures!

◀ There are many styles of cages to choose from. This cage comes with its own ornate stand, making it a bit more decorative.

CAGES

Cages are made of wire, which is either galvanized or coated. It is recommended that you avoid cages that are coated with plastic because the lovebirds may be able to strip the coating. The cage should be equipped with a few perches of different diameters, which will help keep your birds feet strong and healthy. They should be wood, either dowels or natural branches, not plastic.

◀ Most birds love swings as a part of their decor. They favor it as a sleeping perch because it is the highest roosting spot available.

▲ This cage is suitable for this lovebird pair, as it offers enough room for the birds to stretch their wings, but it should have an extra perch or two.

Natural branches are the preferred choice. You can purchase them from pet stores or gather them yourself. They should be green branches, preferably of fruit trees (except cherry) and/or willow trees. Make sure the branches have not been sprayed with any insecticides.

▲ A ladder in the cage will give the bird a chance for exercise. It may be better if hung from the side cage bars resting on one of the perches. It will be less likely to get soiled from droppings.

AVIARIES

Aviaries come in different styles and sizes and the one that will best suit your needs may change along with your goals and ambitions in your aviculture career. The first thing to determine is the location for your structure. It is best if it is visible from the house and situated facing the south. The latter offers more protection from the wind and provides the birds with the most sunlight during the morning hours when they are most active.

The shape of an aviary can be any that you desire, but a rectangular shape is most often used. It is easy to build around and add to if wishing to expand.

The aviary should not be constructed under trees where other birds and animals are able to perch above the flight area and antagonize its patrons. The enclosed shelter is best if constructed from bricks, but wood is also used. The roof should be on a slant. The flight area should sit firmly on the foundation with no open areas.

Part of the flight area should be covered with some sort of Plexiglas sheets or weatherproof material for protection against bad weather. ▶

Perches in the aviary should be of different widths and can be either natural branches or dowels. Natural branches are preferred because they satisfy their urge to chew, and they can strip the bark to use as nesting material. It also helps to keep the beak and nails trim.

Any aviary area can be decorated on the outside with flowers and shrubs. They should not be placed inside because they will soon be chewed up and covered with droppings, making the area appear dirty and sloppy.

◀ Aviaries consist of a sheltered area and a flight area. The shelter should be insulated and have a source of heat. A light should also be included because the birds will not like going from a sunny area to a darkened area. The most preferred ground covering is concrete. It is easy to clean and lasts a long time with little maintenance. A dirt floor is harder to keep clean and promotes bacteria growth. A covering of wire prevents any unwanted guests from burrowing in. Tile or gravel may also be used.

NUTRITION

Feeding lovebirds require more than just filling their seed cups daily. Each bird can have different eating habits and requirements depending on the life it leads and its individual likes and dislikes.

It is very important to purchase a quality mix with various seed types. A cockatiel mix is good because it has slightly larger seeds, such as sunflower, rather than a small seed mixture for budgerigars. Many mixes are sprinkled with vitamins but supplements can be added to the drinking water.

↟ Just because we give our birds a good seed mixture does not mean that they will eat all that is offered. Like ourselves, they will eat what they like first and may surpass other choices that are necessary.

Especially in the summer, offer fresh foods in early morning or evening so that it does not stay out all day in the sun getting sour or drying up. Some food items can spoil easily and the unused portions need to be removed before long. ▪

Lovebirds are constant eaters. Make sure they always have a supply of seed at their disposal. It is important to not just look at the seed cup to see when it needs filling for it may be filled with just the hulls. Take the dish out and blow or shake out the hulls and add fresh. Fruits, berries, vegetables, hard boiled eggs, pasta, rice, and leafy plants may all be fed in addition to the seed diet. Dried greens which are also suitable to offer your birds can be purchased at pet shops.

This bird is in excellent health. To prevent him from becoming overweight, limiting foods high in fat may be necessary. Such foods that could be limited are peanut butter, sunflower seeds and cheese. However, aviary birds will need the added calories. ◆

Plants are toxic if exposed to gas fumes and insecticides. Wash all fresh fruits, vegetables, and leafy greens before feeding them to your birds, especially if collected from the yard. ▶

◆ There are many different packaged treats available. Some are in wheels or sticks held together by ingredients such as honey. They are a welcome item that the birds can gnaw on and will keep them entertained.

NUTRITION

Mashes can also be made by mixing together a variety of ingredients for your bird's delight. These are best offered to aviary birds which are outside year 'round and to breeding hens to ensure they get the extra nutrition they need. Breeding birds expend enormous amounts of energy nest building, incubating, and rearing their young.

◀ A varied diet is the most important requirement for a nutritionally sound bird.

NUTRITION

Supplying your bird with a cuttlebone will help it keep its beak trim as well as supply it with salt and calcium.

In the winter it may be necessary to supply extra calories to help keep them warm and in good condition throughout the colder season. If they receive a varied diet daily, a vitamin supplement may not be necessary. Another dietary supplement that can be supplied is that of soaked seeds. These seeds become more vitamin rich when they begin to germinate, and most birds seem to gobble them up with enthusiasm. These are good for the ailing bird because they are easier on the digestive system.To prepare them soak the seeds in water for 24 hours, then take the seeds and rinse thoroughly before feeding to your birds.

Beside solid food, your bird should always be supplied with fresh clean water. Grit is also an important part of the birds diet. It aids in breaking down seed for easy digestion as well as providing minerals that the bird may otherwise be lacking. A mineral block also aids in digestion and helps make sure no mineral deficiencies occur. All of these ingredients together help provide you with a healthy and well nourished bird.

Do not feed your bird just one type of seed because you see that it is his favorite, variety is the key to good nutrition. However, you may occasionally want to offer a favorite seed as an extra treat.

AS A PET

There are a few things that you should be aware of to keep your new pet healthy and happy.

The first thing to consider is where to place the cage for your new companion. It is good to place it where the bird can observe the daily goings on about the household. Place in an area where it can get natural light, but not directly in front a window or door. You must be careful of drafts for they can make your birds sick, causing colds and asthma. Do not let the cage sit in bright sunlight throughout the day and do not place the cage in the kitchen. The constant fumes are not healthy and it is a dangerous area. God forbid your bird gets loose and flies into a boiling pot of stew!

If your bird is loose, make sure other pets are not around. The first instinct of any dog or cat will be to chase and try to catch the bird. ◗

Birds like to go to sleep just after sundown and wake up with the first rays of light. ▶

Inside pets will not be as hardy as aviary specimens. ➥

Don't forget to equip the cage with the essentials like feed and water dishes, appropriate perches of different widths of either natural tree branches such as willow and manzanita, or wooden dowels, a swing and some toys.

Watch out for household plants that your bird may come in contact with for they may be poisonous. ▶

If properly cared for, your birds will remain healthy and content. ➥

AS A PET

If unconfined, windows should be closed and preferably covered with shears or blinds to prevent the bird from flying into any glass and injuring itself. ◀

Once home, let the bird get used to its new environment by keeping it in the cage for about the first week or two, or at least until the bird is eating well and not showing signs of nervousness or stress. At night you may want to cover the cage to give the bird some quiet time in which to rest without being disturbed.

It is not a good idea to bring your bird outside if not confined. Even if the wings are clipped, a good wind can come along and carry it just far enough away to be in the road or neighbor's yard where a dog or cat might be loose. ▼

You may want to bring your bird outside in the spring and summer to get some fresh air and sunshine. Place the cage in a safe location and where the bird can retreat into shade if the sun is too much. ➤

These birds are not talkers, but if you have the time and patience you can train it to do simple tricks. ▶

Make sure you do not let the bird out and leave it unattended. It is a curious creature and will undoubtedly get into anything and everything. They love to gnaw, so watch out for your furniture and woodwork and do not let the bird near any wiring or cords.

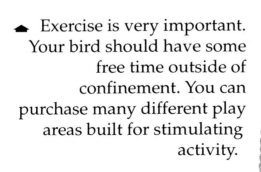

◆ Exercise is very important. Your bird should have some free time outside of confinement. You can purchase many different play areas built for stimulating activity.

◆ When purchasing toys, make sure they are suitable for lovebirds.

GENERAL CARE

When going about the process of cleaning the cage and you do not wish to remove the bird, use only a sponge and warm water. A thorough cleaning with detergents involves removing the bird from its cage so as not to make it ill. Cage bottoms are removable so you can always do a thorough job, they should be cleaned more often than the rest of the cage. Perches should be cleaned weekly. Sandpaper is useful for removing dried droppings from the perches. When washing the dishware, make sure that the seed cup is dried thoroughly if it is damp the seed will become moldy.

Cleanliness is a very important to maintaining your birds health and well being. ◀

You can buy bird baths to fit on the inside or outside of your cage, a shallow dish will also do. ▸

When the weather is cold, be sure that the cage and its contents are dry before replacing the bird so that it does not catch a chill.

The cage bottom should be cleaned often. If using paper for the lining, it is best to replace it daily. Other cage linings such as wood shavings or corncob absorb the moisture and can be changed every few days. Remove any fresh food that has dropped to the bottom daily so it does not spoil or attract bugs. Fresh fruits and vegetables become harmful to the bird if rotted and soiled.

Most birds enjoy a bath so much that some try to fit into their water dish. Bathing helps keep feathers clean. In the summer your bird can bathe more often, but be sure that it is dry before evening so as not to catch a chill.

◂ Offer baths on sunny days for your birds enjoyment.

GENERAL CARE

Not all birds nails require clipping. If it is supplied with a varied diet, fresh branches, and cuttlebone it will remain healthy and active and will naturally wear down its nails. If you see that they are getting a bit long, you may be able to file down the tips with a nail file. If not, a pair of sharp nail clippers will do the job. Some keep styptic powder on hand just in case you cut too far and hit the vein. If you have a nervous bird, having someone assist by holding the bird will make it easier. If you cut a vein press the tip of the nail into the powder. It will be painful to the bird so put it back in its cage and finish the job at another time. Beaks can also become overgrown. You will probably want vet assistance with the beak and maybe even the nails if unsure.

◆ Trimming nails, beak or wings will be easier if you have a bird that trusts you completely.

Always check to make sure the nails are not getting too long. They can create hazardous situations by getting caught up in open areas, on loose threads, and also on the cage wire.

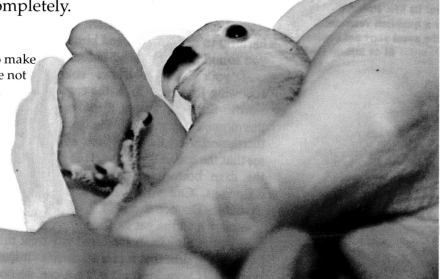

44

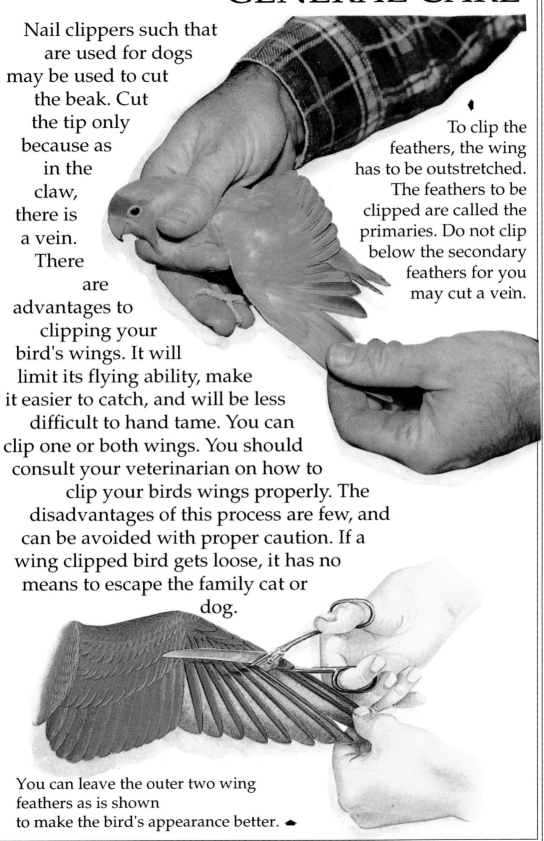

Nail clippers such that are used for dogs may be used to cut the beak. Cut the tip only because as in the claw, there is a vein. There are advantages to clipping your bird's wings. It will limit its flying ability, make it easier to catch, and will be less difficult to hand tame. You can clip one or both wings. You should consult your veterinarian on how to clip your birds wings properly. The disadvantages of this process are few, and can be avoided with proper caution. If a wing clipped bird gets loose, it has no means to escape the family cat or dog.

To clip the feathers, the wing has to be outstretched. The feathers to be clipped are called the primaries. Do not clip below the secondary feathers for you may cut a vein.

You can leave the outer two wing feathers as is shown to make the bird's appearance better. ◄

HEALTH CARE

Being prepared for any accident or illness will make it easier for you to handle any situation that may arise. Accidents and injuries are only a few issues to be concerned with as well as moulting, feather plucking and veterinarian care.

Your bird may become injured if frightened by flying into a wall, window, or against the sides of its cage. If this should happen, put the bird in a hospital cage, if available, to limit its activity. The bird may be in shock, so it is important to keep it warm.

▲ This bird will renew its plumage yearly through the moulting process. During this time you will not notice any gaps in the feathers. This process happens quite smoothly.

Your bird will be easier to handle in an emergency if it is hand tame. ▲

◀ Vitamin and mineral supplements will benefit birds during their moult. Their resistance is low during this time.

Providing this bird with twigs to gnaw on, as well as other toys, a varied diet, and a clean environment, should prevent feather plucking problems. ▶

Remove the perches so it can rest on the cage floor. Not much else can be done except to bring it to the vet to splint any broken bones. If your bird should receive a severe wound, it should be taken to the vet immediately. A small wound can be treated with an antiseptic or styptic stick. Another health issue is feather plucking. This can occur from different causes such as boredom, nutritional deficiencies, unsuitable climate, psychological disturbances, skin ailment or even another bird. You may not readily know the cause. Try offering other playthings as well as spending more time with the bird and checking its diet. If these actions fail consult your vet.

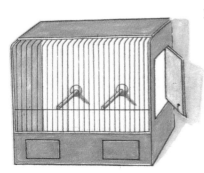

◀ An extra small cage is handy to have around if your bird should become ill or injured.

Sometimes a cage mate can be responsible for wounding the other. Try to determine what happened so that you can prevent the same thing from occurring twice. ▶

SEXING AND PAIRING

The Black-winged Lovebird leaves no question as to its sex; the male has a red forehead. Finding a compatible mate is the next step to a successful brood. ▶

It is not easy to determine the sex of lovebirds unless they happen to be one of the three dimporhic species, these being the Madagascar Lovebird, the Red-faced Lovebird and the Black-winged Lovebird. It is unfortunate, however, that the three most popular species are monomorphic, meaning that both sexes are alike. There is a method in which a veterinarian can surgically determine the sex. This is done usually only with larger birds.

◆ These Peach-faced Lovebirds may seem a compatible couple, but only time will tell. There is the possibility that they could be of the same sex.

The only way to really determine the sex is through observation of mating and the egg hatching of a pair.

◀ When obtaining a pair of lovebirds for breeding, do not acquire birds from the same clutch. Inbreeding can produce weak and unhealthy young.

SEXING AND PAIRING

Some breeders will put a small group of birds together and closely monitor their behavior to see if pairs are formed. This gives the birds an opportunity to choose their own mates, but severe fighting may also occur.

If acquiring only one pair, be sure that you can exchange one of the birds if it does not prove to be a pair. It may be wise to obtain proven pairs if you find them available. Otherwise you will have to wait to develop your own proven breeding stock.

The birds that have paired should be moved to their own aviary. If colony breeding, remove the birds that have not paired. There should be more nest boxes than pairs situated throughout the compound and they should have ample space apart from each other.

NESTING

Be careful not to make the opening of the nest box too large. If it is too small, they will whittle away at it to make the adjustment. ◗

The lovebird is a cavity nester. In the wild they build nests in hollow tree cavities or use old bird nest sites. A box size of about 7x8x10 in.is suitable for the larger species and a little less for the smaller species. The box should be made of a thick wood. Do not use pressboard because they will chew holes through it easily. A perch should be placed a little below the nest box opening on the outside. Inside, a ladder made of wooden slats should be placed below the entrance hole. This will make it easier for the hen and chicks to climb out of the box.

The roof should have a hinged top to make nest inspection easier. ◄

Softer nesting materials are used by the birds lacking the white eye ring. They construct soft, little, cup shaped bottoms to lay their eggs on.

◗

◄ Nesting materials should be offered three to four weeks before you expect the hen to lay her eggs. At this time she will begin building her nest, and she will continue to add to it throughout the incubation period.

Fischer's Lovebird will often nest in umbrella acacias, like these, in their native homeland. ▶

The opening is best if placed to one side, which will limit the sunlight, and should be just large enough for the lovebirds to get in and out. It will give them a sense of security.

It is important to provide your birds with an over abundant amount of materials in which to build their nests. Offer plenty of fresh twigs, dried grasses, dried and fresh leaves, and other non poisonous plant cuttings. When hanging the nest boxes, place them in a covered area in shady, secluded sites. Two boxes per pair are recommended because it will give them the opportunity to choose their own nesting site. When breeding in a colony system, try to hang the boxes in similar areas and at similar heights so that there is not a lot of squabbling over the more preferred nest sites.

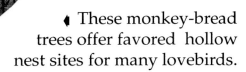

◀ These monkey-bread trees offer favored hollow nest sites for many lovebirds.

EGG LAYING

Lovebirds will lay an average of 3 to 5 eggs per clutch which are white in color. Eggs are usually laid every other day, but incubation will not take place until the second or third egg is laid. During the incubation period the male feeds the female so that she does not have to leave the nest unguarded. However, she may occasionally leave to stretch her wings or gather some more nesting material.

◆ Incubation is almost always the sole responsibility of the hen. The cock will usually join the hen in the evening, snuggling close to her throughout the night.

◆ Lovebirds can lay anywhere from 1 to 8 eggs, but if more than five are laid, all will not hatch.

An average incubation period is between 21 and 25 days, but this may vary slightly depending on the species and the temperature.

Chicks of sexually dimorphic species, such as the Red-faced, Madagascar, and Black-winged Lovebird, are covered with white down. Chicks of monomorphic species are covered in red down. ◆

Chicks are supplied with a sharp egg tooth at the tip of their beaks to aid them in cutting through the shell during hatching. ➤

A couple days before the chick emerges, you may be able to hear some cheeping coming from inside the egg as well as the tapping sounds made by its beak in its first attempts at release. The success of hatching depends largely on having the proper humidity. If moisture is too low, they can die within the egg before being fully developed, or the eggs will become hard and the the chicks will not be able to break out. This can be avoided by supplying plenty of fresh green twigs with which they will continually shred and put around the eggs, as well as supplying a bird bath. The birds will bathe and bring moisture into the nest, or the nest box can be moistened daily, depending on how dry your conditions are. Be careful that the water is not too cool and do not soak the nest box because the chicks inside the eggs could drown.

◀ Newly hatched chicks are bald and their eyes are closed. Within a few days they have some fuzzy down to help protect them from the cold.

CHICK REARING

During the period of chick rearing, the impor- tance of an added variety of seed, greens,

◀ Not all birds will tolerate intrusions into the nest box for inspections.

This bird has already acquired its fuzzy down.
➡

fruits and an ample amount of soft high protein food mashes can not be stressed enough . These items help the parents give their chicks the best nutritional meals.During this time, the cock continues to help feed the hen as well as the chicks. The chicks will be dependent upon their parents for about 5 weeks. As soon as the chicks leave the nest, they begin the weaning process. The cock will still feed the chicks for the next week or two after fledging.

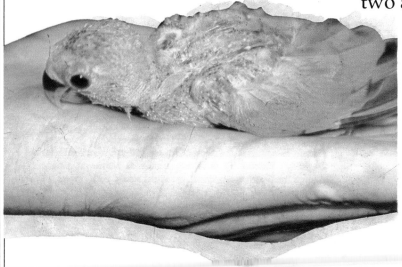

◀This chick has had its feathers plucked by the parents. Reasons for this could be diet, low humidity, or boredom.

CHICK REARING

→ A hand fed chick will make a tame and trusting companion.

Even after the chicks have left the nest they will return to it in the evening to sleep. This will not last long. The hen will usually be getting ready for another clutch as soon as her chicks have fledged. At this point it is important to keep a close watch that the parents do not start to attack the youngsters. If this is the case, remove the youngsters immediately. After removal from the parents, it is still important to supply the chicks with soft food as well as seed. At first, they will only play with the seed, while continuing to eat the soft food. It does not take long before they take completely to the seed diet.

← These 30 day old Red-faced Lovebird chicks are already used to being handled.

◀ Chicks will have almost complete plumage by the time they are 3 to 4 weeks old.

TAMING AND TRAINING

→ The wings should be clipped for the taming process. It will make it easier on you and your bird.

If one wants a very tame and affectionate lovebird, a hand-raised baby is the best buy. An older bird will be much more difficult to train, although it is not impossible. A few things you will need to start with are a wooden dowel about a foot long, a quiet room where there are no distractions, and if you feel it necessary- gloves. It is best if you do not use the latter because they more often frighten the bird. However, their bite can be nasty. If wearing gloves, make sure they are snug fitting, smooth, and light or flesh color. The training area should be a room that is as uncluttered as possible with very little or no furniture. This will make retrieving the bird

▲ It is important before you start the taming process that the bird has had time to adjust to its new surroundings. Give the bird at least one to two weeks to settle in.

easier. All mirrors and windows should be covered, and doors closed.

By maintaining daily taming sessions, it will not be long before the bird will voluntarily let you pet it. The bird may even let you teach it a few tricks. ◀

TAMING AND TRAINING

Young birds can be distinguished by the black coloring of the beak. ▶

If utilizing a small area, the bird will not have very far to go to get away from you. It will soon get used to your close presence. Next, you will want to take the dowel and put it up to the bird nudging it lightly on its chest to make it step up onto the perch. It will probably try to fly away, but if the wings are clipped, it should not be able to go far. Avoid chasing after the bird with the dowel because the bird may become frightened and injure itself. Wait until the bird has settled and repeat this process. You will only want to work with the bird for about fifteen minutes then take a break. This will let both of you regroup. You may want to do a few sessions per day, but at first do not exceed one hour.

◄ Remember, do not get frustrated, always remain calm and use a soothing gentle tone when talking to your new companion.

If acquiring a hand-raised youngster, it will already be used to some handling. It will easily turn out to be a very tame and trusting companion. With a young bird, the training process should be fairly quick. ◀

TAMING AND TRAINING

The glove pictured here will probably frighten the bird because it is big and bulky, unlike a hand. If gloves are going to be used at all, make sure they are smooth and form fitting. ▸

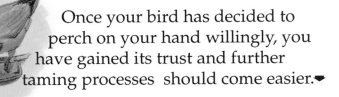

When the bird is on the perch, bring your hand slowly up to its chest pressing lightly so that he will have to step up onto your hand. ➤

Once your bird has decided to perch on your hand willingly, you have gained its trust and further taming processes should come easier. ➤

➤ With time and patience, your bird will enjoy perching on your hand or shoulder. This allows the bird more freedom. Now he can be taken out to join you for a bit of play time, or to keep you company about the house.

After teaching your bird to perch on a dowel, you will want to get it to perch on your finger or hand. This will be done in the same manner as teaching it to perch on a dowel.

Banding takes place when the chicks are about six days old. If any rings appear too tight, a trip to the vet for removal is required.

The reason for banding chicks is for identification. The bands are dated so the age can be determined as well as other coded information, such as its sex.

There are two types of bands, plastic and metal. The plastic is not recommended for lovebirds because they can easily destroy them. The metal closed bands are permanent once fitted. Close watch must be kept at first to make sure the band does not constrict blood flow. This could result in the loss of a foot.

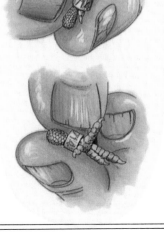

To put the bands on, slip it over the forward toes. Hold the rear toes even with the shank and gently push the band up the shank area. Ease the rear toes, one at a time, through the band. The use of some petroleum jelly will help the toes slip through.

DISEASE AND ILLNESS

The first step to treating any disease or illness in a bird is to learn how to recognize if it is sick. This bird is not feeling well. ▸

In order to recognize any signs of illness, it is important to know your bird and how it usually behaves. If no symptoms are recognized until the bird is clearly in distress, it is usually too late. The first sign a bird may exhibit when ill is the loss of appetite. If this is noticed, there should be no hesitation in consulting a vet. If any warning signs are ignored for a few days, a minor illness can become a major one. Other clinical signs can be loss of weight, labored breathing, sitting with feathers fluffed, diarrhea, discharge from the nostrils, and runny eyes.

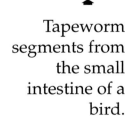

Tapeworm segments from the small intestine of a bird.

◂ This bird shows all signs of being alert and healthy.

DISEASE AND ILLNESS

◀ These are feather lice shown attached to the underside of a wing.

Because there are many illnesses that are hard to diagnose in birds, blood and fecal specimens may be necessary to help the vet attain a diagnosis. Many illnesses bring about the same symptoms, so an avian vet should be contacted right away. External parasites include feather lice, mange mites, and red mites. If a bird is infected with large numbers of these parasites, it can be a major concern and can lead to death. Such infestations can be prevented through regular cleaning and disinfecting procedures.

◀ A magnified picture of a typical biting louse.

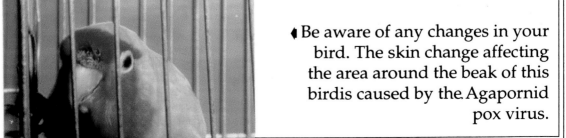

◀ Be aware of any changes in your bird. The skin change affecting the area around the beak of this birdis caused by the Agapornid pox virus.

DISEASE AND ILLNESS

Tapeworm infestations will more likely occur in aviary birds so it is important that they are checked yearly for any such problems. ▸

Internal parasites are not common in house birds if kept clean, but are more likely to occur in aviary birds. If a bird is found over eating but losing weight or has stopped eating altogether, it may be a sign of such infestations. These can be cured with veterinarian prescribed medications. It is advisable to have fecal matter examined yearly in aviary birds because sometimes there are no noticeable signs of a problem until the death of a bird.

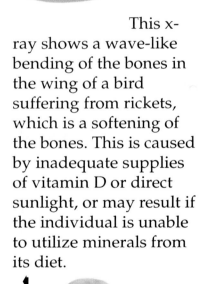

This x-ray shows a wave-like bending of the bones in the wing of a bird suffering from rickets, which is a softening of the bones. This is caused by inadequate supplies of vitamin D or direct sunlight, or may result if the individual is unable to utilize minerals from its diet. ◂

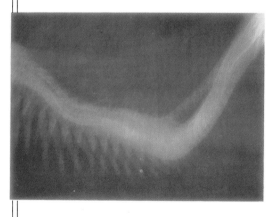

Through environment and diet, rickets can be avoided. If this bird gets exposure to sunlight daily, as well as vitamin and mineral supplements, it should not suffer from this ailment. ▸

DISEASE AND ILLNESS

This bird is going through a breast examination.

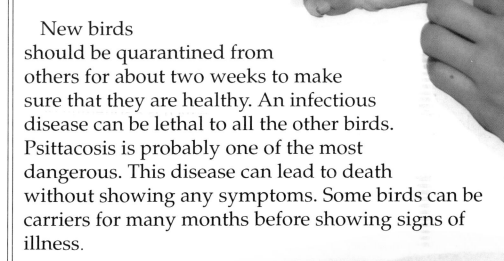

Sometimes certain ailments require surgical procedures. This bird is being restrained with tape before undergoing anesthesia.

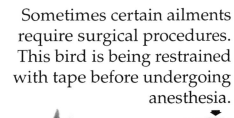

New birds should be quarantined from others for about two weeks to make sure that they are healthy. An infectious disease can be lethal to all the other birds. Psittacosis is probably one of the most dangerous. This disease can lead to death without showing any symptoms. Some birds can be carriers for many months before showing signs of illness.

This cheerful looking bird is showing no signs of illness. Hopefully your bird will stay bright and healthy throughout its lifetime. ◗

INDEX

Page numbers in **boldface** refer to illustrations.

Accidents, 46
Agapornid pox virus, **61**
Agapornis cana, 10–11
Agapornis fischeri, 22–23
Agapornis lilianae, 20–21, **27**
Agapornis nigrigenis, 19
Agapornis personata, **5**, 24–25
Agapornis pullaria, 12–13
Agapornis roseicollis, **5**, 16–17, **48**
Agapornis swinderniana, 18
Agapornis taranta, 14–15, **48**
American Pied Light Green Peach-faced Lovebird, **27**
American White Peach-faced Lovebird, **28**, **29**
Aviaries, 32–33, **32**, **33**
Banding, 59, **59**
Bathing, 43, **43**
Beak trimming, 44
Black-cheeked Lovebird, 19
Black-collared Lovebird, 18
Black-winged Lovebird, 14–15, **48**
Blue Masked Lovebird, **25**, **26**
Cages, 30–31, **30**, **31**
Cages, placement of, 38
Chick rearing, 54–55
Cinnamon Blue Peach-faced Lovebird, **29**
Cinnamon Peach-faced Lovebird, **28**
Cinnamon Slate Peach-faced Lovebird, **29**
Cobalt Peach-faced Lovebird, **29**
Cremino Peach-faced Lovebird, **28**
Dutch Blue Peach-faced Lovebird, **26**
Egg laying, 52
Feather lice, **60**, **61**

Feather plucking, 47, **54**
Fischer's Lovebird, 22–23
Hatching, 53
Illness, recognizing, 60
Incubation, 52
Life-span, 4
Lutino Nyasa Lovebird, **20**, **27**
Lutino Peach-faced Lovebird, **28**, **29**
Madagascar Lovebird, 10–11
Masked Lovebird, **5**, 24–25
Mutations, 26–29
Nail clipping, 44
Nest boxes, 50, **50**
Nesting, 50–51
Nutrition, 34–37
Nyasa Lovebird, 20–21, **27**
Orange Peach-faced Lovebird, **27**
Pairing, 48–49
Parasites, 61
Peach-faced Lovebird, **5**, 16–17, **48**
Perches, 33, 38
Pied Dutch Blue Peach-faced Lovebird, **29**
Pied Peach-faced Lovebird, **4**
Psittacosis, 63
Red-faced Lovebird, **7**, 12–13, **55**
Rickets, **62**
Selection, 6–9
Sexing–48-49
Silver Cherry Peach-faced Lovebird, **27**
Soaked seed, 36
Taming, 56–58
Tapeworms, **60**
Toys, **41**
Wing clipping, 45, **45**
Yellow Fischer's Lovebird, **26**
Yellow Peach-faced Lovebird, **29**